EAST ANGLIAN DAILY TIMES   Evening Star

IPSWICH TOWN FC
The 1980s

WOULD YOU LIKE ONE OF THE IMAGES IN THIS BOOK?

To order a copy of any of the classic photographs within this book, and to view many others, go to www.eadt.co.uk/myphotos24 or telephone Sharon Clark on 01473 324813

EveningStar EAST ANGLIAN DAILY TIMES

EAST ANGLIAN DAILY TIMES **Evening Star**

IPSWICH TOWN FC
The 1980s

TERRY HUNT

First published in Great Britain in 2011 by
The Derby Books Publishing Company Limited,
3 The Parker Centre, Derby, DE21 4SZ.

This paperback edition published in Great Britain in 2014 by
DB Publishing, an imprint of JMD Media Ltd

© Archant Regional, 2011

All Rights Reserved. No part of this publication may be
reproduced, stored in a retrieval system, or transmitted in any
form, or by any means, electronic, mechanical, photocopying,
recording or otherwise without the prior permission in writing of
the copyright holders, nor be otherwise circulated in any form or
binding or cover other than in which it is published and without a
similar condition being imposed on the subsequent publisher.

ISBN 978-1-78091-393-3

Printed and bound in the UK by Copytech (UK) Ltd Peterborough

Contents

Foreword	7
1979–80: Building towards glory	8
1980-81: The greatest season	16
1981-82: Robson's final campaign	52
1982-83: Decline sets in	76
1983-84: 'Boys doing men's jobs.'	90
1984-85: A relegation dogfight	100
1985-86: The dreaded drop	116
1986-87: Play-off disappointment	135
1987-88: Duncan era begins	153
1988-89: Treading water	172
1989-90: Fans turn on the boss	185

Foreword

The 1980s began in sublime fashion for Ipswich Town.

1980-81 was, arguably, the club's greatest campaign, as Bobby Robson's team fought on three fronts – the League, the FA Cup, and the UEFA Cup.

Producing brilliant football – were they the best side in Europe? – they eventually paid the price for playing so many games and were forced to settle for the 'consolation prize' of the UEFA Cup. Some consolation prize!

We Town fans thought this would last forever. After all, Ipswich had been one of the top teams for a decade now, so why shouldn't these great days continue?

We had a team full of internationals, except for goalkeeper Paul Cooper, whose best years unfortunately coincided with the peak of Peter Shilton and Ray Clemence. Surely there was yet more glory ahead?

But it unravelled so quickly. In 1982, Robson was snapped up by England, following in the footsteps of Sir Alf Ramsey. Under Bobby Ferguson's management, the great side started to break up, and all too quickly Town began to struggle.

The departing stars were not adequately replaced, money wasn't available, and a very sad decline set in. In 1986, with a team unrecognisable from that which triumphed in Europe only five years earlier, Town tumbled out of the top flight. Who will ever forget Terry Butcher's tears?

Ferguson paid the price for failing to restore Ipswich to Division One at the first attempt, and was replaced by John Duncan, whose three-year tenure at Portman Road will not be remembered with any great affection. It was as much the dour style of football as the lack of success which alienated fans. After all, Ipswich has always had the finest tradition of playing football the way it should be played.

Duncan's time ended with the unthinkable – Ipswich fans demanding a manager's head. Town remained a mediocre Division Two side, and it was all too hard to take for a generation of fans brought up on the Robson glory years. It was all so different to the glorious way in which the decade had started for the team and its supporters.

It would take the arrival of John Lyall to restore some pride and success – but that's for another decade, and another book.

Terry Hunt

1979–80: Building towards glory

The building blocks were being put in place: Bobby Robson had his two Dutchmen running midfield, Alan Brazil had broken through, Eric Gates had established himself in the first team, and Terry Butcher and Russell Osman had replaced the stalwarts Hunter and Beattie.

Although this was a successful season in its own right – third in the League and FA Cup quarter-finals are not to be sniffed at – it was nothing compared to what was to come the following year.

Division One final position: third
FA Cup: Quarter-final
League Cup: Second round
UEFA Cup: Second round

Gary Bailey is about to save Kevin Beattie's penalty in the 6–0 win over Manchester United – one of three spot-kicks he stopped.

1979-80: Building towards glory

Not a picture you see very often – Bobby Robson signing a player. Robson famously bought very few players during his 13 years at Portman Road, preferring to bring them through the ranks. It worked pretty well! This is Robson watching as Kevin O'Callaghan puts pen to paper after signing from Millwall at the beginning of 1980. Town paid what was then a club record £200,000. Although never a regular, O'Callaghan was to play his part.

Paul Mariner has just scored one of his hat-trick goals against Manchester United at Portman Road in March 1980.

Youngsters of today won't believed that this happened…It's March 1980 and Town are on their way to beating 'mighty' Manchester United 6–0. This is one of Alan Brazil's two goals, Paul Mariner got a hat-trick and Frans Thijssen scored the other. Amazingly, United 'keeper Gary Bailey also saved three penalties!

1979-80: Building towards glory

Kevin Beattie makes a rare appearance against Derby in March 1980. The game ended 1–1, with Eric Gates on target for Ipswich. Paul Cooper's reputation as a spot-kick stopper continued to grow – he saved two penalties in this match.

Norwich 'keeper Roger Hansbury braves John Wark's boot in this Easter Monday game in 1980. Town run out 4–2 winners with Wark scoring a hat-trick, including two penalties. Paul Mariner is the other Ipswich scorer.

Wrong way, Roger! 'Keeper Hansbury is beaten by John Wark's spot-kick during Town's 4–2 win over Norwich in April 1980.

Ipswich squeezed past Bristol City 2–1 at Aston Gate in the fourth round of the FA Cup in 1980. Paul Mariner scored a late winner, with John Wark the other Town scorer.

1979-80: Building towards glory

Eric Gates tries his luck in characteristic style in the FA Cup fourth round tie against Bristol City at Ashton Gate. 'Gatesy' was out of luck this time, but Town came home with a 2–1 win.

Funny old game, football. In February 1980, high-flying Ipswich took on struggling Brighton at Portman Road. A home win, surely? It looked that way as John Wark put the home side ahead from the penalty spot. But there was a dramatic twist of fate. On came Suffolk-born Gary Stevens as substitute, against the club which had released him. Here's our Gary, being skinned by Alan Brazil. But in the very last minute, with Ipswich still leading 1–0, guess what happened? You're right – Stevens popped in the equaliser.

Frans Thijssen is about to receive his Player of the Year award from Patrick Cobbold in this picture from April 1980.

1980-81: The greatest season

This campaign is often described as Town's greatest but, in truth, it was a bitter-sweet mixture, despite their triumph in Europe.

Ipswich fought on three fronts for most of the season, playing a mammoth number of games in their bid to capture a unique treble of League Championship, FA Cup, and UEFA Cup.

In the end, perhaps inevitably, injuries took their toll on Bobby Robson's small squad, and Town were pipped at the post in the League by Aston Villa, who ironically had been beaten at Portman Road in the third round of the FA Cup, thus leaving the Midlanders to concentrate on the League.

The Blues also suffered heartbreak in the semi-final of the Cup, with a Paul Power free-kick in extra-time ending their hopes. That game marked Kevin Beattie's last appearance for the club.

But, of course, Ipswich did enjoy glory in Europe, with victory in the UEFA Cup, after a glorious run in which John Wark scored no fewer than 14 goals.

So, they had something to show for a remarkable season.

Division One final position: Runners-up

FA Cup: Semi-final

League Cup: Fourth round

UEFA Cup: Winners

The opening day of a memorable season: John Wark celebrates after scoring a late winner at Leicester in the first game of the 1980–81 campaign. Sixty-six games later, Town won the UEFA Cup, and there were lots of highs and lows in between.

1980-81: The greatest season

The famous footballing phrase 'Twisted Blood' comes instantly to mind when seeing Frans Thijssen with the ball at his feet. That's what his opponents would suffer as they were mesmerised by yet another mazy dribble. This is the Dutchman in action against Everton in August 1980.

A moment of anxiety in the home game against Everton in August 1980. They needn't have worried – Town walloped the visitors 4–0 with goals from Brazil, Wark, Butcher and Mariner.

The first of three games against Aston Villa in 1980–81, two in the League and one in the FA Cup. Town won them all, but Villa won the League – how did that happen? Ipswich won this early season encounter 1–0 with Frans Thijssen the scorer.

Frans Thijssen is congratulated after scoring the only goal of the game against Aston Villa at Portman Road in September 1980. Town would go on to beat Villa three times that season – twice in the League and once in the FA Cup – but the Midlands side had the last laugh. Staying clear of the injuries which afflicted Town, and with far fewer games to play, they won the Division One Championship. Town's failure to win the League that year was one of Bobby Robson's biggest footballing disappointments.

1980-81: The greatest season

Alan Brazil fires in a cross during the 3–0 UEFA Cup win over Bohemians of Prague in October 1980.

A small squad, a massive fixture list and injuries eventually put paid to Town's treble ambitions in the extraordinary 1980–81 season. In all, Ipswich played 66 games with Russell Osman the only ever-present. Inevitably, the injuries began to mount up, and the squad was too small to withstand them. Solid but unspectacular squad players such as Robin Turner were not of the necessary quality. Here, Turner challenges West Brom's Ally Robertson in a 0–0 draw in November 1980.

Town players signing club annuals, Christmas 1980. From the left are Paul Mariner, Frans Thijssen, Eric Gates, Steve McCall and Paul Cooper.

Canaries 'keeper Roger Hansbury dashes from his line to foil John Wark during the League Cup third round replay at Carrow Road in October 1980. Hansbury couldn't stop Town progressing with a 3–1 win, with two goals from Mariner and one from Muhren.

Eric Gates and Kevin O'Callaghan seem to be enjoying smashing a bottle stuffed with charity money at an Ipswich pub in December 1980.

Penalty king John Wark dispatches another one successfully to earn Ipswich a point at fellow title chasers Arsenal at Highbury just after Christmas 1980. Alan Sunderland, later to turn out for Town, had put the Gunners ahead.

Paul Mariner celebrates one of the best goals ever seen at Portman Road. A sublime move involving five players ended with Mariner firing the ball home to secure a 1–0 win for Town against Aston Villa in the third round of the FA Cup in January 1981. But, brilliant though the goal was, did it prove fatal to Town's hopes of winning a unique treble that memorable season? Being knocked out of the Cup at the first hurdle allowed Villa to concentrate on the League, whereas Ipswich were fighting on three fronts, and eventually injuries and fixture congestion took their toll – although the UEFA Cup did find its way to Portman Road!

It looks for all the world like an archetypal John Wark goal, but the camera can lie sometimes. This game against Everton at Goodison Park in January 1981 ended goalless.

1980-81: The greatest season

Three legends celebrate: Franz Thijssen and Paul Mariner congratulate John Wark on opening the scoring in a 5–1 trouncing of Birmingham on a freezing night in January 1981.

Eric Gates is congratulated by John Wark after scoring one of his two goals against Shrewsbury in the FA Cup fourth round replay at Portman Road in January 1981. Town win 3–0, with Wark the other scorer.

Paul Mariner celebrates one of the Ipswich goals in a comprehensive 4–0 thumping of Stoke City in January 1981. Mariner himself wasn't on target – the goals came from Brazil (two), Wark and Gates. Stoke 'keeper Peter Fox is appealing in vain for an infringement.

1980-81: The greatest season

Paul Cooper flies through the air with the greatest of ease against Liverpool at Anfield in October 1980. The game ended 1–1, Thijssen scoring for Town.

The maestro Kenny Dalglish looks like he's got the beating of George Burley at Anfield in October 1980 during a 1–1 draw. Mind you, Burley's got plenty of help, with Osman, Muhren and Thijssen close by.

Everything comes your way when you're one of the top teams in Europe. Mick Mills taking delivery of a load of oranges in February 1981. There's more than enough for half-time, lads!

Gatesy has wriggled his way past another defender and the alarm bells are ringing for Crystal Palace at Portman Road in February 1981. Ipswich won this encounter 3–2, with goals from Mariner, a Wark penalty and an own-goal from visiting defender Gilbert.

1980-81: The greatest season

A very familiar sight at Portman Road in the early 1980s. The ball in the back of the net, the 'keeper nowhere to be seen, and John Wark celebrating yet another successful penalty. This one was in a 3–2 win over Crystal Palace in February 1981.

Kevin Beattie looks like he's missed a sitter in this FA Cup fifth round tie against Charlton at Portman Road in February 1981. No matter – Town won 2–0 with Wark and Mariner on target.

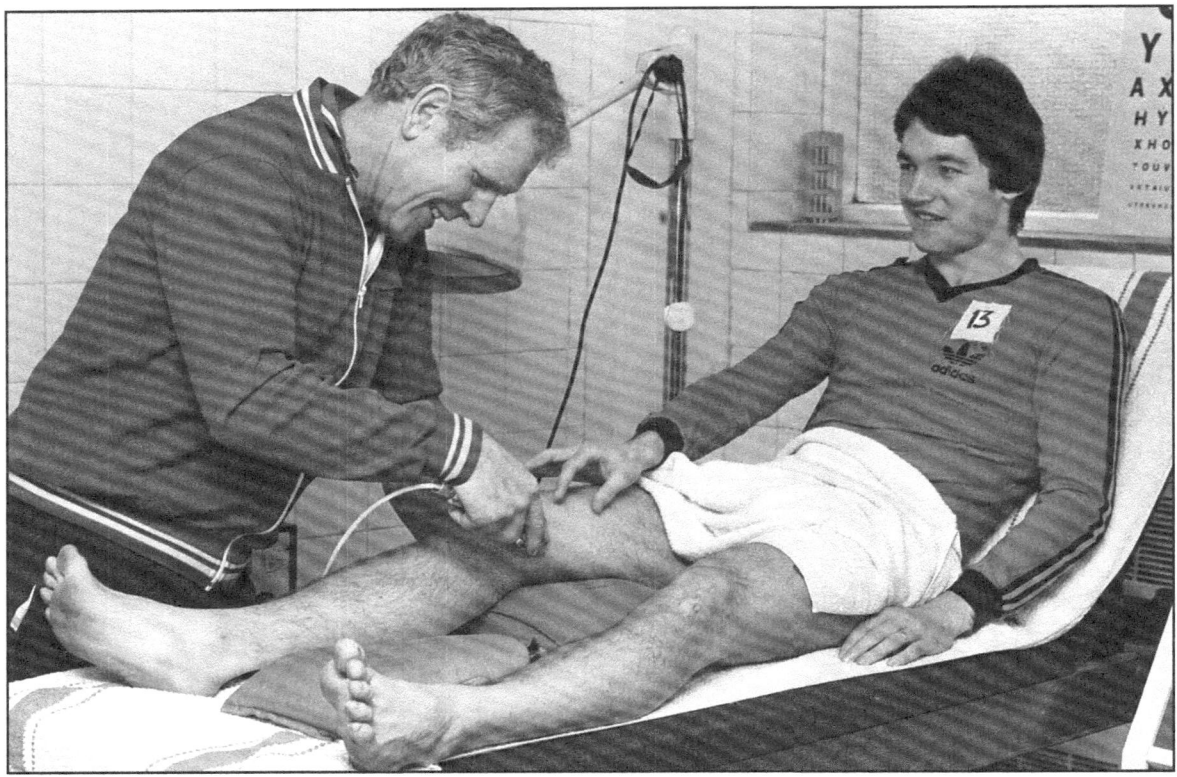

George Burley suffered a career-threatening knee injury halfway through the 1980–81 season, which robbed him of the chance to play in the UEFA Cup Final. It all seems pretty relaxed in this picture as Burley undergoes treatment. Perhaps the number on his shirt summed up his season.

Mind me head! Alan Brazil ducks out of the way of a clearance as Town take on Middlesbrough in February 1981. Brazil had the last laugh – he scored the winner.

1980-81: The greatest season

Eric Gates and Kevin O'Callaghan signing autographs for young fans before Town's memorable UEFA Cup tie against St Etienne – Michel Platini and all. What followed was arguably the greatest Ipswich performance of them all – a 4–1 away win at the home of one of Europe's best sides.

A spot of keepy uppy outside the hotel to while away the time before a UEFA Cup match. Pictured are Eric Gates, Russell Osman, Paul Cooper, Kevin O'Callaghan and Alan Brazil.

Peter Shilton is beaten as Frans Thijssen's deflected shot squirms its way into the net to earn Town a 3–3 draw in the FA Cup quarter-final against Forest in 1981. Paul Mariner and Terry Butcher seem quite pleased.

Players leave the pitch, headed by Kevin O'Callaghan, after the inconclusive FA Cup quarter-final against Nottingham Forest in March 1981. Town won the replay.

A rare moment – Arnold Muhren scoring with his right foot! This was the spectacular winner in the FA Cup quarter-final replay against Nottingham Forest.

Town fans are fenced in during the FA Cup quarter-final against Forest at the City Ground in March 1981. Those who had a decent view witnessed a 3–3 thriller.

1980-81: The greatest season

John Wark with the Footballer of the Year trophy in March 1981. A top honour, thoroughly well deserved.

1980-81: The greatest season

Alan Brazil is a study in concentration during Town's League clash with Spurs at Portman Road in March 1981. Brazil was one of the scorers in a 3–0 victory, with Wark and Gates also on target.

Barry Daines is given no chance as John Wark buries yet another penalty high into the roof of the net during Town's 3–0 win over Spurs in March 1981. The phenomenal Scot would score 36 times that season – from midfield.

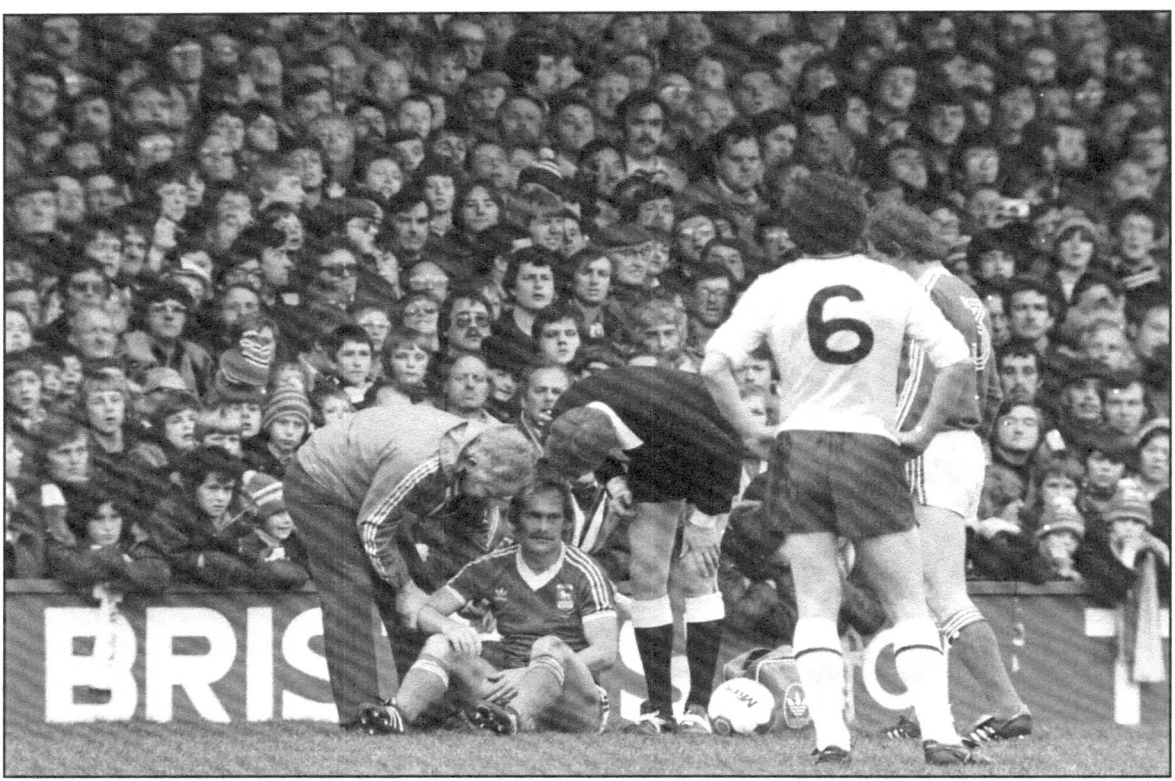

Town skipper Mick Mills suffered a rare injury – a dislocated shoulder – during the 3–0 win over Spurs in March 1981. He would miss the next two games.

Terry Butcher celebrates after putting Town one up at Old Trafford in March 1981. However, Manchester United came back to win the game with goals from Micky Thomas and Jimmy Nicholl. It was a dent in Town's title ambitions.

Gordon McQueen (now better known to fans of Sky Sports) clears the ball from Paul Mariner during Town's 2–1 defeat at Old Trafford in March 1981. Eric Gates and John Wark are the other Ipswich players in the foreground, along with Manchester United 'keeper Gary Bailey, son of Town legend Roy.

Ipswich fans looking anxious during the first leg of the UEFA Cup semi-final against Cologne in 1981. They needn't have worried…

Yet another Manager of the Month award for Bobby Robson, this one during the memorable 1980–81 season.

1980-81: The greatest season

We're in the Final! Goal hero Terry Butcher celebrates the UEFA Cup semi-final victory over Cologne.

Ouch, that hurt! But Alan Brazil's momentary discomfort in this collision with Manchester City 'keeper Joe Corrigan isn't nearly as bad as the pain of losing in the semi-final of the FA Cup.

Ipswich fans at the FA Cup semi-final against Manchester City at Villa Park in April 1981. Paul Power's free-kick in extra-time spelled heartbreak for the travelling supporters, and the team.

1980-81: The greatest season

The saddest picture of them all. A stricken Kevin Beattie leaves the pitch for the last time as an Ipswich Town player. After battling a succession of knee injuries, ironically it was a broken arm in the FA Cup semi-final against Manchester City in 1981 that spelled the end for a player who is consistently voted as Town's greatest. An injury-free Beattie would surely have won 100 England caps and gone on to establish himself as an all-time great of the game. The fact that he won only nine caps remains one of the game's cruellest injustices. It was a privilege to have watched him play at his peak.

Just three days after heading Town's winner in Cologne to put them through to the UEFA Cup Final, Terry Butcher does it again, this time with the only goal of the game against Manchester City at Portman Road. The dream is still alive…

We're on our way to Amsterdam. Town fans ready to leave for the UEFA Cup Final in May 1981. They would come back happy.

The match officials look relaxed, but Mick Mills has an apprehensive frown as he leads Ipswich out for the second leg of the UEFA Cup Final in Amsterdam.

Mick Mills gives his AZ Alkmaar counterpart the eye before the start of the UEFA Cup Final second leg in Amsterdam in 1981. After a few scares, Town came through.

The Town team wave to the visiting fans before the UEFA Cup Final second leg.

Tense times. Substitutes Tommy Parkin, Kevin O'Callaghan and Robin Turner watch the action during the second leg of the UEFA Cup Final. Bobby Robson looks worried too.

Well, there's a surprise! John Wark has just scored his 14th goal in Town's UEFA Cup run in 1980–81. This one just happened to be in the second leg of the Final.

1980-81: The greatest season

Come on you Blues! Ipswich fans enjoying the Amsterdam sunshine during the second leg of the UEFA Cup Final.

Ipswich Town's best-ever squad? These were the players who came so close to pulling off a remarkable treble in the 1980–81 season, winning the UEFA Cup, finishing runners-up in the League, and losing in the semi-final of the FA Cup.

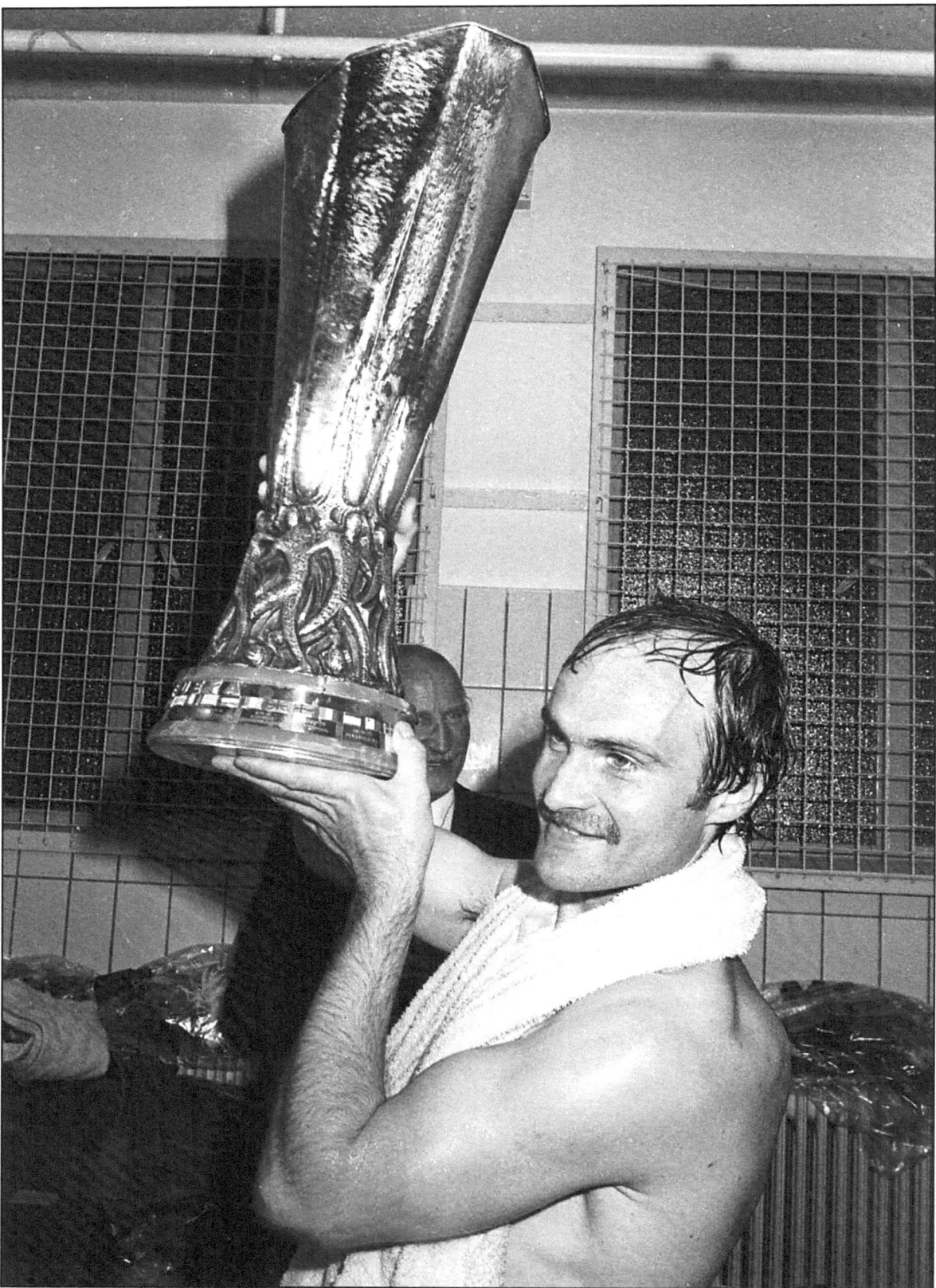

The iconic picture of Town skipper Mick Mills with the UEFA Cup after the victory over AZ Alkmaar. The giant Cup is almost as big as Millsy!

1980-81: The greatest season

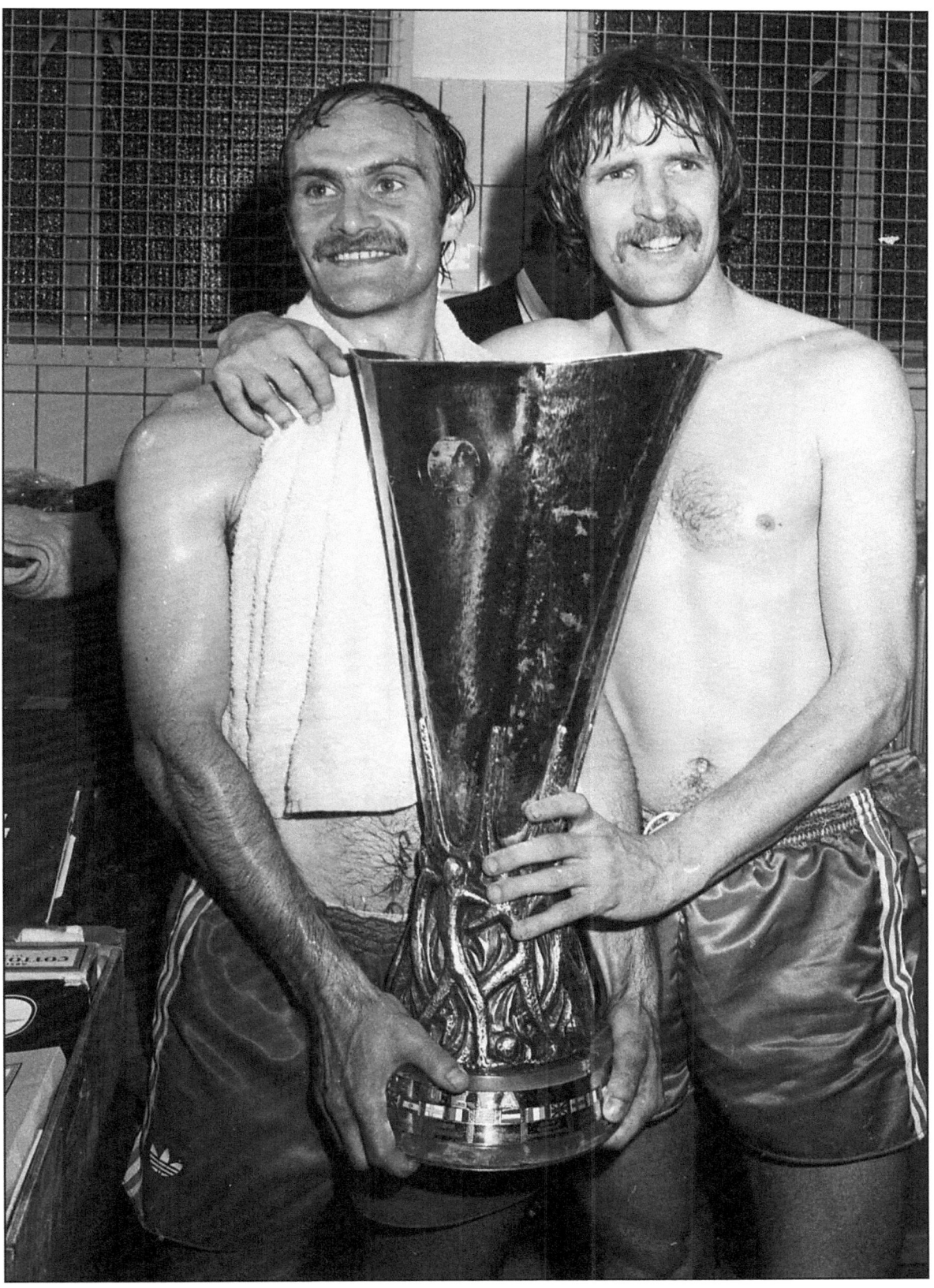

Mick Mills and Frans Thijssen with the UEFA Cup after a tense second leg in Amsterdam, during which Town had to protect a slender single goal lead for the final 20 minutes.

Nice pants, Paul! Mariner and John Wark celebrate winning the UEFA Cup.

Leading the UEFA Cup celebrations, May 1981.

IPSWICH TOWN The 1980s

Fans mob the open-topped bus as Town players proudly show off the UEFA Cup.

1980-81: The greatest season

1981-82: Robson's final campaign

In what was to be Bobby Robson's last Ipswich campaign, Town once again came agonisingly close to bringing more silverware back to Portman Road, but ultimately it was a season of frustration.

Town finished runners-up to Liverpool in Division One, but serious injuries to key men Terry Butcher and Frans Thijssen weakened the challenge. The Dutchman played only 12 League games.

The Blues made it through to the semi-finals of the League Cup for the first time, but were well beaten by Liverpool over two legs.

In the UEFA Cup, holders Ipswich were shocked in the first round by Alex Ferguson's superb Aberdeen team, inspired by Gordon Strachan, who beat Town 4–2 on aggregate.

Highlights of the season included Alan Brazil's extraordinary five-goal salvo against Southampton. 'Pele' was Town's top scorer with 28 goals.

After a fantastic 13-year reign, Bobby Robson left to take the England job, following the same route as Alf Ramsey nearly 20 years earlier. It truly was the end of an era.

Division One final position: Runners-up

FA Cup: Fifth round

League Cup: Semi-final

UEFA Cup: First round

These fans were treated to a six-goal thriller at Portman Road on the opening day of the 1981–82 season, Town drawing 3–3 with Sunderland. Wark, and Gates with two, were the scorers.

1981-82: Robson's final campaign

A bearded Terry Butcher training hard. Butcher's defensive partnership with Russell Osman was at the very heart of Town's successes in the early 1980s. Were they better than Hunter and Beattie? The arguments go on!

Town are UEFA Cup holders, and skipper Mick Mills joins a young fan to leaf through a souvenir book.

In control, as always. Arnold Muhren on the ball during a 2–1 Town win over Leeds at Portman Road in September 1981. Terry Butcher and Eric Gates were on target.

Arnold Muhren holds off a tenacious Arthur Graham as Town take on Leeds at Portman Road in September 1981.

1981-82: Robson's final campaign

Eric Gates in action against Southampton at The Dell in October 1981. Town let a 3–1 lead slip to lose 4–3, and a furious Bobby Robson describes it as his worst result for 10 years.

No wonder Butcher and Mariner look grumpy. Town are 3–1 up at half-time at Southampton in October 1981, but end up losing 4–3. Wark (two) and Mariner are the Ipswich scorers.

A guard of honour for Allan Hunter as he takes to the field for his testimonial game against Celtic in November 1981. The Irishman had given 10 years' service to Ipswich after becoming one of the most important signings Bobby Robson ever made. The Celtic supporters shorted the lights by relieving themselves in the North Stand!

1981-82: Robson's final campaign

Ipswich beat relegation-bound Wolves 1–0 at Portman Road in October 1981, with Kevin O'Callaghan scoring his first for the club. Here, John Wark challenges for a cross.

Another pinpoint pass leaves the incomparable left foot of Arnold Muhren as Town take on surprise packets Swansea at Portman Road in November 1981. The Welsh side left Portman Road with a 3–2 win despite goals from Muhren and Mariner.

1981-82: Robson's final campaign

Alan Brazil looks like he's offering a prayer of thanks after Paul Mariner equalises against Swansea at Portman Road in November 1981. But the Welsh side won the game 3–2.

After 10 months out with a career-threatening knee injury, George Burley made a welcome return to the first team in a League Cup tie against Bradford in November 1981. It wasn't a memorable match, with Ipswich being held 1–1 by the Fourth Division team, but Town won the replay 3–2.

Town players training in the snow in January 1982. Among the hardy souls are, from left, Laurie Sivell, Alan Brazil, Steve McCall, Terry Butcher and John Wark. Boss Bobby Robson can just be glimpsed in the background.

An amazing achievement. Mick Mills and teammates celebrate the skipper's 700th game for the club in January 1982. His record will surely never be beaten.

They say that Bobby Robson did everything at Portman Road – and here's the proof. Fork in hand, the Town manager checks the pitch before a game in January 1982. Club secretary David Rose looks on.

Struggling Notts County stunned Town by coming to Portman Road and winning 3–1 in January 1982, Frans Thijssen netting the consolation goal. The Dutchman is seen being congratulated by Steve McCall.

A rare moment indeed – a headed goal from Frans Thijssen. This was the only bright spot in an otherwise dismal performance against Notts County at Portman Road in January 1982. A 3–1 defeat was a body blow to hopes of winning the League.

A youthful Alan Hansen fails to stop Eric Gates firing in a cross at Anfield in February 1982. Centre-half turned consummate TV pundit Hansen and his teammates had the last laugh all round – they won this game 4–0 and pipped Town to the Division One title.

Paul Cooper and Kenny Dalglish leave the pitch after Town are thumped 4–0 by Liverpool at Anfield in February 1982. Inevitably, Dalglish was on target.

Eric Gates has just scored against Liverpool at Anfield in the League Cup in February 1982, but the celebrations are a tad muted. That's because Ipswich have already lost the first leg 2–0, and are also two goals behind in this leg with time running out. To their credit, they managed a draw in this game, with a second goal coming from Alan Brazil.

Bobby Robson receives a Team of the Month award in February 1982 from former FIFA President Sir Stanley Rous.

How many's that, Pele? Arnold Muhren congratulates Alan Brazil during the striker's amazing five-goal spree against Southampton at Portman Road in February 1982. The number nine running away from camera is Mich D'Avray, who set up several of Brazil's goals. Town won 5–2.

1981-82: Robson's final campaign

Johnny on the spot again. Wark fires home one of Town's goals in a 3–0 win over Everton at Portman Road in March 1982. The others come from Alan Brazil and Eric Gates.

Farewell to a legend – Town take on Moscow Dynamo in Kevin Beattie's testimonial game in March 1982. Here. Beattie gives Ipswich fans a glimpse of his old, inimitable style.

All hands to the pump as Aston Villa defend in numbers against Ipswich in March 1982. Town won this encounter at Portman Road courtesy of goals from Wark, McCall and Gates.

These young fans are having a great time as Town play Brighton in March 1982. No wonder – Ipswich won 3–1.

Mich D'Avray looks determined to get to the ball first against Brighton in this game at Portman Road in March 1982. Town won 3–1, with two goals from Brazil and one from Wark. Brighton's Steve Foster can be seen sporting his distinctive headband.

A rare sight indeed – an Arnold Muhren header! The Dutchman was always much happier when the ball was on the ground. Paul Mariner and West Ham's David Cross watch in amazement during this game at Portman Road in April 1982, which Town won 3–2. Brazil, Wark and Osman were the scorers.

Alan Brazil starts his goal celebration in characteristic style after putting Town ahead in a thriller against West Ham at Portman Road in April 1982. Phil Parkes is the grounded 'keeper. The game ended 3–2 to Ipswich, with Brazil and Wark the other scorers for the home side, and David Cross getting both for the Hammers. Games against the East End outfit always seemed to provide lots of goals and plenty of entertainment.

Although not as prolific as in the previous season, John Wark nonetheless scored 23 times during the 1981–82 season – not bad for a midfield player! Here the Scot has just scored one of his two goals in the 2–1 win over Manchester United at Portman Road in April 1982. Eric Gates is helping him celebrate. This game was notable for featuring the only Town appearance for veteran 'keeper John Jackson.

1981-82: Robson's final campaign

Town took on Manchester City in April 1982. The game ended 1–1, with Alan Brazil on target, but behind that scoreline lies a remarkable story – John Wark missed a penalty. Now, that didn't happen very often.

Town pair Terry Butcher and Paul Mariner battle for the ball with Tommy Caton and Kevin Bond in this game against Manchester City at Maine Road in April 1982. It ended 1–1, with Alan Brazil on target for Town. John Wark and Russell Osman await the outcome of this aerial battle.

Old heroes. An Ipswich Town players' reunion at Portman Road in April 1982. Chairman Patrick Cobbold welcomes the former players.

1981-82: Robson's final campaign

John Wark scores in spectacular fashion for Town's first in a 3–1 home win against Middlesbrough in May 1982. Muhren and Brazil were also on target, but ultimately it's another season of disappointment for the Blues. They finish runners-up in the League for the second consecutive year, four points behind champions Liverpool, and fail to make any impact in the Cups.

Four Town greats. Mariner, Gates, Muhren and Wark celebrate the Dutchman's superb free-kick against Middlesbrough in May 1982. It was to be Muhren's last Town goal. He left for Manchester United at the end of the season, and the rot began to set in. Town won this game 3–1, with Wark and Brazil also on target.

1981-82: Robson's final campaign

Action from Town's last game at Portman Road under Bobby Robson. Ipswich won the final League game of the 1981–82 season 2–1 against Spurs, with Mick Mills and Alan Brazil the scorers. Tottenham's consolation came from Garth Crooks, now better known as a TV pundit. Here,. Crooks' fellow striker Steve Archibald is dispossessed by Terry Butcher.

Action from Bobby Robson's last game as manager of Ipswich Town. A 2–1 home win against Spurs brought down the curtain on the 13-year Robson era.

John Cobbold presents the Player of the Year trophy to Alan Brazil in May 1982. The young Scots striker had a phenomenal season, scoring 28 goals.

1981-82: Robson's final campaign

1982-83: Decline sets in

Under new boss Bobby Ferguson, Town's final League placing of ninth was their worst since 1971–72, apart from the FA Cup winning campaign of 1977–78.

The great team of 1981 began to break up with Arnold Muhren, Mick Mills, Frans Thijssen and Alan Brazil all leaving either before or during the season. Mills' departure was particularly poignant, after 17 years and a record number of appearances.

Town never really recovered from a terrible start, with no wins in their first six League games.

Ipswich were knocked out of the UEFA Cup by Roma in the first round. It would be a long time before Ipswich fans enjoyed European competition again.

There were also early exits from both the FA Cup (a painful defeat at Norwich) and the Milk Cup.

Highlights included a club record 6–0 away win at Notts County. Wark was top scorer with 23 goals.

Division One final position: Ninth
FA Cup: Fifth round
Milk Cup: Second round
UEFA Cup: First round

Players and other staff at Portman Road say goodbye to Bobby Robson as he leaves to take up the England job in August 1982.

1982-83: Decline sets in

A sad, but proud day. John Cobbold says goodbye to Bobby Robson as the legendary Town manager leaves to take up the England post in August 1982. During 13 years at Portman Road, Robson had transformed Ipswich from perpetual Division One strugglers into one of the best teams in Europe, winning the FA Cup, the UEFA Cup, and coming agonisingly close to the League Championship on a number of occasions. Of course, Robson was following in the footsteps of another former Ipswich manager, Sir Alf Ramsey. He so very nearly repeated Ramsey's feat of winning the World Cup.

Alan Brazil celebrates in trademark style after putting Town ahead against Spurs at Portman Road in the first home game of the 1982–83 season. But Spurs hit back to win the game 2–1.

1982-83: Decline sets in

Alan Brazil gives Town the lead against Spurs in September 1982. Tottenham must have been impressed – they bought him later in the season. The Londoners came back to win this one 2–1 to get Town's home campaign off to a disappointing start.

A fine action study of Steve McCall, a versatile left-sided player who served Ipswich Town for many seasons, including deputising for the badly injured George Burley in the second half of the memorable 1980–81 season.

1982-83: Decline sets in

The post-Robson era didn't start well for Town in the 1982–83 season. They didn't win any of their first six League games. In the third game of the season, Coventry grabbed a point in a 1–1 draw with a late goal after Paul Mariner put the home side ahead. Here's the Town goal with John Wark following it into the net.

Alan 'Pele' Brazil in action at Old Trafford against Manchester United in September 1982. Town lost 3–1 to continue their desperately diappointing start to the season. Later in his career, Brazil joined the Red Devils.

Mich D'Avray battling against AS Roma in the UEFA Cup in September 1982. Town made an early exit from a competition they had won two seasons earlier.

Ipswich's hopes of a long UEFA Cup run in 1982–83 came a cropper when AS Roma saw them off. The Italians establish a three goal lead from the first leg, and a brave effort by Ipswich in the second leg at Portman Road wasn't enough. Town win the second game 3–1, with goals from Eric Gates, Steve McCall – seen here trying his luck – and Terry Butcher.

1982-83: Decline sets in

Diving Eric Gates looks as though he's scored against Liverpool in October 1982, but the referee Mr Lewis has his whistle to his lips. Town did win this game, however, thanks to a brilliant header from Mich D'Avray, thus ending the Reds' 23-match unbeaten run.

Stand-in striker Mich D'Avray only played against Liverpool in October 1982 due to injury to Paul Mariner and Alan Brazil's illness. But he had a great day, powering home an 81st minute header to win the game.

New faces were being introduced at Portman Road during the 1982–83 season. Here's Irvin Gernon in action in the home defeat aganst Arsenal in October 1982.

Steve McCall has just given Tony Woodcock the brush-off as Town take on the Gunners in October 1982. But England striker Woodcock had the last laugh, scoring the only goal of the game.

1982-83: Decline sets in

The home League game against Arsenal at Portman Road in October 1982 proves to be Mick Mills' last appearance for Town in front of the home fans. It was a forgettable way for his magnificent Ipswich career to end – a 1–0 defeat, courtesy of Tony Woodcock's second half goal.

Action from Town's memorable 6–1 thrashing of West Brom in October 1982. John Wark helped himself to four of the goals, with others coming from Gates and Thijssen.

John Wark helps Eric Gates to celebrate his goal in the 6–1 trouncing of West Brom in October 1982. Wark got four himself!

A score to please all Town fans. Ipswich pulverised West Brom in October 1982.

Town were struggling in this FA Cup third round clash against Charlton at the Valley in January 1983, finding themselves two goals down in the first 15 minutes. But a Frans Thijssen volley and a controversial penalty from John Wark levelled things. Wark steals the win in the last minute. The picture shows Paul Mariner challenging for the ball.

He went that a-way! Kevin O'Callaghan tries to mesmerise a Grimsby defender in this FA Cup fourth round game at Portman Road in January 1983. Ipswich won 2–1 with goals from Osman and McCall. The saddest sight of the day was former Ipswich striker Trevor Whymark being stretchered off after suffering a serious knee injury after only two minutes.

Action from a disappointing FA Cup clash with local rivals Norwich City at Carrow Road in February 1983. The Canaries won the game with an early goal from former Town striker Keith Bertschin, who can be seen here on the right of the picture. Another future Town striker, John Deehan, is also waiting to pounce as Ipswich defend desperately.

Trevor Putney was one of Town's goalscorers in this 3–1 win over Birmingham in March 1983. Alan Brazil, also pictured, finished off his Portman Road career with a goal before departing for Spurs. Russell Osman was the other scorer.

1982-83: Decline sets in

Alan Brazil scored twice against his old teammates when Ipswich went to White Hart Lane in April 1983. Spurs won the game 3–1, with Paul Mariner getting Town's consolation. Here, Brazil pits his wits against Kevin Steggles.

Teammates help John Wark to celebrate one of his two goals in the final home game of the season against Watford in May 1982. The Hornets finish second in the table, but are well beaten 3–1 by Town, with the other goal coming from Steve McCall.

1983-84: 'Boys doing men's jobs'

The above was a quote from manager Bobby Ferguson as his squad was left threadbare with the departure of more star names.

This time it's the iconic Paul Mariner and John Wark heading for the pastures new, both leaving after an unfortunate and very public pay dispute.

Town finish in mid-table but the final table hides the truth. For much of the season, Ipswich were struggling against the very real threat of relegation, before a late revival saw them pull clear.

Ipswich lost embarrassingly to lowly Shrewsbury in the FA Cup, and there was more misery at the hands of local rivals Norwich City, a Mike Channon goal beating Town in the fourth round of the League Cup.

A definite highlight was the debut goal for Ipswich schoolboy Jason Dozzell, becoming the youngest Division One scorer at just 16 years and 57 days.

Division One final position: 12th
FA Cup: Fourth round
Milk Cup: Fourth round

John Wark notched his sixth hat-trick for Town in the thrilling 4–3 Milk Cup second round first leg at Portman Road in October 1983. Here he is, celebrating in typical fashion.

1983-84: 'Boys doing men's jobs'

Leicester 'keeper Mark Wallington thwarts John Wark during this dull 0–0 draw at Portman Road in October 1983. Paul Mariner is on hand. Both Wark and Mariner were involved in a pay dispute with the club.

Back of the net! Unfortunately, Paul Mariner hasn't taken the ball with him during a 0–0 draw with Leicester at Portman Road in October 1983.

IPSWICH TOWN The 1980s

John Wark and Paul Mariner are rightly regarded as Ipswich Town icons, but there was a time when they weren't so popular with some supporters. A row blew up in 1983 when both players demanded pay rises and fell out with management. The episode dragged on, and led to sections of supporters showing their feelings, hence this banner at the Milk Cup game

against Queen's Park Rangers in November 1983. Credit where credit's due, it was normal service from Wark and Mariner, with both on the scoresheet as Ipswich won this third round game 3–2.

After joining Ipswich from Plymouth in 1976, Paul Mariner gave the club great service and became England's centre-forward. He featured prominently in both the FA Cup and UEFA Cup winning sides. He remains a hero at Portman Road, as was shown when he returned as Plymouth manager. But the manner of his departure during the 1983–84 season was unfortunate. Mariner and John Wark were both dubbed 'pay rebels' after a dispute with management over their salaries. Mariner eventually moved to Arsenal in early 1984. Here he is, in action against the Gunners a few months earlier, in November 1983. Town won this game 1–0, thanks to a goal from Eric Gates.

The crowd of 12,900 for Town's game with Birmingham at Portman Road in January 1984 was the lowest for 17 years. It would get worse before the decade was out…The diehards didn't have much to cheer about, either. Birmingham won the game 2–1, with Terry Butcher's own-goal proving decisive. Mich D'Avray had put Ipswich ahead. Here, Kevin O'Callaghan comes up against a wall of Birmingham defenders.

Alan Sunderland arrived on loan from Arsenal in February 1984. Sunderland had sealed his place in the hearts of Gunners fans with his dramatic last-gasp winner against Manchester United in the 1979 FA Cup Final. Town supporters will not have such fond memories of him, although he did play his part in saving Ipswich from relegation in his first season at Portman Road by scoring a late goal at Old Trafford with, ahem, an interesting part of his anatomy.

Foiled again. The ball is safely in the arms of Birmingham 'keeper Tony Coton during the Midlanders' 2–1 win at Portman Road in January 1984.

Ipswich came a cropper against their 'hoodoo' side Shrewsbury in the FA Cup in 1984, losing 2–0 at Gay Meadow in the fourth round. It was the third time in four seasons they had lost to the lower League team.

1983-84: 'Boys doing men's jobs'

Terry Butcher and John Wark put the Coventry defence under pressure at Portman Road in February 1984. Ipswich won 3–1, in a game when 16-year-old Jason Dozzell made his historic goalscoring debut.

A memorable debut which still holds its place in the record books. Ipswich schoolboy Jason Dozzell, pictured here on that day, was 16 years and 57 days old when he came on as substitute against Coventry at Portman Road on 4 February 1984. A minute from the end of normal time, the fairytale came true and Dozzell fired home Town's third goal to become the youngest goalscorer in English football's top flight. Despite the best efforts of the likes of Wayne Rooney, that record still stands. Dozzell, of course, went on to have an illustrious career with Ipswich and later Spurs. Town won this game 3–1 with Mariner and Brennan also on target. It was Mariner's final game before joining Arsenal.

Alan Sunderland in action during Town's dismal 3–0 home defeat against West Ham in March 1984. Things were looking grim, but a seven-match unbeaten run at the end of the season lifted the Blues to mid-table safety.

Great players were leaving and being replaced by lesser lights. Town were on the decline. Here, Trevor Putney and Tommy Parkin battle for the ball in a crushing 3–0 home defeat at the hands of West Ham in March 1984.

1983-84: 'Boys doing men's jobs'

It looks for all the world as though this must be a Mich D'Avray goal against visitors Sunderland in May 1984. But it wasn't – Russell Osman scored the only goal in a 1–0 Town win.

'A team of boys doing men's jobs' is how manager Bobby Ferguson described his side as they battled away in the 1983–84 season. They certainly finished the campaign well, unbeaten in their last seven games to end up 12th in the table. Part of that unbeaten run was this 1–0 win over Sunderland. Here, Russell Osman celebrates his winning goal.

1984-85: A relegation dogfight

Struggling Ipswich spent long spells of the season in the bottom three, but, once again, saved themselves with a late-season revival. They finished a single point outside the relegation zone, while neighbours Norwich went down after winning the Milk Cup.

Eric Gates took over the mantle of top goalscorer, with the mid season arrival of bustling Kevin Wilson also helping on the goalscoring front.

But the break-up of the great UEFA Cup-winning team continued, with Eric Gates, Russell Osman and George Burley all playing their last games for the club in this season. Without being cruel, their replacements were not of the same quality and there was a definite feeling of decline.

There was yet more heartbreak at the hands of Norwich in the Milk Cup, with Steve Bruce heading a dramatic last-gasp winner in the semi-final second leg at Carrow Road. The Canaries went on to lift the trophy, although they were relegated.

In the FA Cup, Town went on a good run, which was only ended at the quarter-final stage by Everton.

Division One final position: 17th

FA Cup: Quarter-final

Milk Cup: Semi-final

Alan Sunderland didn't score too many goals for Ipswich, but here's one of his best as he beats Kevin Moran to a cross and heads Town's equaliser against Manchester United in September 1984.

1984-85: A relegation dogfight

Gary Bailey is beaten as Alan Sunderland scores against Manchester United.

Town's first win of the 1984–85 season came courtesy of a 2–1 victory over Arsenal at Portman Road in September, thanks to goals from Russell Osman and Romeo Zondervan. Here, Trevor Putney looks like he's just been on the receiving end of a right hook from Mike Tyson! In the background is former Ipswich hero Brian Talbot.

Russell Osman is congratulated after scoring one of Town's goals in a 2–1 win over Arsenal at Portman Road in September 1984. Tommy Caton seems to be pointing something out rather forcefully to his downcast teammates, including Brian Talbot.

The likely lads: Mark Grew and Frank Yallop in 1985. Grew never really established himself, but Yallop went on to play more than 300 games for Ipswich.

1984-85: A relegation dogfight

Bristol Rovers had been one of Town's opponents during the memorable 1978 FA Cup run, and they were back in the west country in January 1985. The result was the same, a 2–1 win, thanks to goals from Jason Dozzell and Mark Brennan. Here, Rovers defend a Town free-kick.

Romeo Zondervan on the ball during Town's narrow 3–2 win over Gillingham in the FA Cup fourth round at Portman Road in January 1985. Goals from Kevin Wilson, Jason Dozzell, and an own-goal secured the win. Town reached the quarter-finals before losing to Everton after a replay.

Steve McCall takes the ball away from a Gillingham player during Town's 3–2 FA Cup victory over the Kent side in January 1985.

1984-85: A relegation dogfight

Kevin Wilson celebrates a goal on his debut against Gillingham in this FA Cup third round tie at Portman Road in January 1985. Town won a thriller 3–2.

Ipswich boy Jason Dozzell runs to celebrate with the fans after scoring the winner in Town's 3–2 FA Cup victory over Gillingham in January 1985.

Jason Dozzell is a study of concentration during this Milk Cup game against QPR in January 1985. Town saw off the Londoners after a fifth round replay, only to come a cropper in the semi-final against Norwich.

Tempers flare during a tense night at Carrow Road in March 1985. Town take a slender one goal lead into the second leg of the Milk Cup semi-final, and the evening ends in heartbreak when Steve Bruce heads a late winner from a corner. Hapless substitute Alan Sunderland misses a great chance. Here, shy and retiring Terry Butcher is resolving a difference of opinion with Canaries full-back Dennis Van Wyck. Norwich go on to win the trophy against Sunderland (Chisholm own-goal) but are also relegated.

Eric Gates in the thick of the action as Town take on Newcastle at Portman Road in March 1985. Gates, who was born in the North East, came to the home side's rescue with an 80th minute goal to earn a point. Peter Beardsley and Chris Waddle were in Jack Charlton's Toon team.

Romeo Zondervan is in charge of the situation as Ipswich take on Newcastle at Portman Road in March 1985. The game ended 1–1, with Town salvaging a point thanks to a late goal from Eric Gates.

Mark Brennan bursts past the Bristol Rovers defence during Town's 2–1 FA Cup victory at Eastville in January 1985.

Pick that out of the net! Alan Sunderland's diving header crashes home to give Town the win against Nottingham Forest in April 1985.

Town players Mich D'Avray and Terry Butcher celebrate Alan Sunderland's winner against Nottingham Forest in April 1985. Sunderland himself, number 12, wheels away in triumph. Forest centre-forward Garry Birtles, now a regular football summariser on TV, looks less than thrilled.

There are some notable characters in this action picture from Town's 1–0 win over Nottingham Forest in April 1985. Challenging Mich D'Avray for the ball is none other than Paul Hart – with hair! – while looking on are Garry Birtles and Johnny Metgod.

It looks a bit crowded as Kevin Wilson attempts to get in a shot against Nottingham Forest in April 1985. Paul Hart is about to challenge, while others include Mich D'Avray, Eric Gates and Johnny Metgod.

Shall we dance? Alan Sunderland and Gary Gillespie seem to be ignoring the ball in this Ipswich-Liverpool clash at Portman Road in April 1985. There were no goals.

Ipswich and Spurs fans getting along famously before the game at White Hart Lane in April 1985. These Town supporters were in for a great afternoon, as their struggling team beat high-flying Tottenham 3–2 with goals from Alan Sunderland, Mark Brennan and Eric Gates. A noteworthy result, as Spurs went on to finish third.

Cool, calm, and in control – just like on *Match of the Day*! Alan Hansen sees off Mark Brennan during Town's 0–0 draw with Liverpool at Portman Road in April 1985.

A good action shot of Mark Brennan during the goalless draw against Liverpool in April 1985. Among the young midfielder's illustrious opponents are Phil Neal and Ronnie Whelan.

Kevin Wilson was an instant success at Ipswich, scoring nine times in 15 games in the second half of the season. Three of them came in a 5–1 win against Stoke in May. Here, he celebrates with Trevor Putney, who was on the scoresheet himself. The other Town scorer was Eric Gates. Stoke were having a miserable season. They finished 23 points adrift at the bottom of Division One, with only 17 points and three wins from 42 games.

Stoke 'keeper Barry Siddall has the ball, but it's Town who are celebrating yet another goal during their 5–1 demolition of the visitors from the Potteries in May 1985.

A young fan with his heroes, Tony Butcher and George Burley.

Mid-winter conditions for an end of season game in May 1985. The ball seems almost incidental as players struggle to keep their feet at a quagmire-like Portman Road as Town take on Coventry. Home striker Kevin Wilson is in the thick of the action here. This ended 0–0 and both teams escaped relegation.

1984-85: A relegation dogfight

A filthy night at Portman Road in May 1985, and to make matters worse a dull game against Coventry ended goalless. Here, Paul Cooper, Frank Yallop and Ian Cranson fend off a Coventry attack.

There's no doubt whose ball this is as Terry Butcher rises to head clear during a 0–0 draw against Coventry at the end of the 1984–85 season.

1985-86: The dreaded drop

After 18 years in Division One, Town finally suffered the misery of relegation. Of the glorious side of five years earlier, only Butcher and Cooper were still at Portman Road. All the other stars had gone, and their replacements were either inexperienced or lacking in quality.

Kevin Wilson contributed 15 goals, but no one else came close to double figures.

The bitter end came when Town lost at Sheffield Wednesday, and two days later Oxford beat Arsenal to clamber to safety and condemn Ipswich to the Second Division for the first time since 1968.

Ipswich enjoyed a decent run in the Milk Cup before eventually losing to Liverpool in the quarter-final. In the FA Cup, Ipswich were beaten by West Ham after three tense games.

Lionheart Butcher departed for Glasgow Rangers as Ipswich fans faced up to Second Division football.

Division One final position: 20th

FA Cup: Fourth round

Milk Cup: Quarter-final

After losing their first two games of the 1985–86 season, Ipswich needed to beat Spurs – and they did, thanks to this goal from Romeo Zondervan. The season would end in tears.

Who's the Birmingham 'keeper dealing with this Town attack in September 1985? It's none other than a pre-ponytail David Seaman. Ipswich lost this depressing encounter 1–0, thanks to a goal from Town's Wembley 1978 hero David Geddis.

Worrying times. Alan Sunderland in action during Town's dreadful 3–0 home defeat against Aston Villa in September 1985. Fans chant for manager Bobby Ferguson to be sacked.

Town came back from a goal down to win 3–1 in the first leg of the Milk Cup second round tie against Darlington at Portman Road in September 1985. Kevin Wilson grabbed two, and the other came from Frank Yallop. Ipswich completed the job with a 4–1 victory in the away leg, and went on to reach the quarter-final, where they lost to Liverpool.

He was never going to be a like-for-like replacement for the Dutchmen, Muhren and Thijssen, but Trevor Putney put in many no-nonsense shifts for Ipswich Town. Here's the midfielder in action against Darlington in the Milk Cup in 1985.

1985-86: The dreaded drop

Chelsea gave Ipswich a lesson in finishing when they came to Portman Road in November 1985, Kerry Dixon and David Speedie both netting inside the first 10 minutes. Here, Dixon shields the ball from Romeo Zondervan.

Kevin Wilson wheels away after putting Ipswich ahead in an extraordinary game at Oxford in November 1985. Ipswich are 3–0 up after 53 minutes, with Mark Brennan and Jason Dozzell also on target. But John Aldridge then scores a seven minute hat-trick and the home team score an 80th minute winner. Town are relegated at the end of the season, one point behind Oxford, who saved themselves on the final day.

The *East Anglian Daily Times* scoreboard at Portman Road signals a rare positive during the depressing 1985–86 season. Town end up winning this Milk Cup fourth round tie against Swindon 6–1, with goals from Terry Butcher (two), long-forgotten Michael Cole (also two), Mark Brennan and Kevin Wilson.

A crunching tackle from Town's Mark Brennan during the 2–1 home win against Sheffield Wednesday in November 1985. Mich D'Avray scored twice to give struggling Ipswich a very welcome victory over a decent Owls outfit, who finished the season in the top six.

1985-86: The dreaded drop

South African centre-forward Mich D'Avray was never the most prolific of scorers, and he suffered because he was always compared with the greats like Mariner and Brazil. But here's action from one of his more successful Ipswich games. He scored twice to secure this 2–1 win against Sheffield Wednesday in November 1985.

Jason Dozzell in action during Town's 1–0 win over QPR just before Christmas 1985. Kevin Wilson scored the only goal.

Paul Cooper takes to the pitch for his Testimonial match against Norwich in March 1986. It wasn't the most successful of evenings – only 4,500 people turned up, and Town lost 1–0.

1985-86: The dreaded drop

123

Mark Brennan scores during an extraordinary FA Cup tie against Bradford City in January 1986. The game ends 4–4, with Town's goals from an own-goal, Kevin Wilson, Mark Brennan and Mich D'Avray. Ipswich win the replay 1–0.

Ipswich lost 2–1 at home to Arsenal in March 1986 to increase relegation fears. Here, Mark Brennan is frustrated by a combination of Viv Anderson and the late David Rocastle. Jason Dozzell scored the Ipswich goal.

1985-86: The dreaded drop

Terry Butcher lets fly, and the ball is in the back of the net – the Town skipper's winner against West Brom in March 1986.

Iconic skipper Terry Butcher celebrates his spectacular winner against West Brom at Portman Road in March 1986. This win was a massive boost in Town's relegation battle.

Terry Butcher beats former teammate Alan Brazil in the air. Town beat Coventry 1–0.

Mark Brennan's shot is in the back of the net and Town have beaten Coventry – Alan Brazil and all – in March 1986.

1985-86: The dreaded drop

It's 'squeaky bum time' as the 1985–86 season nears its end. Manchester City are the visitors to Portman Road, and they shut up shop in a goalless draw. Town have five games to save themselves.

Ipswich are finding goals very hard to come by as the relegation trapdoor looms towards the end of the 1985–86 season. A Kevin Sharp goal condemns them to yet another 1–0 defeat at Everton, with only three games left. Here, Jason Dozzell battles in the air.

IPSWICH TOWN The 1980s

Jason Dozzell has just equalised in a thrilling relegation encounter against Oxford in April 1986. Steve Perryman doesn't look happy.

Lionheart Terry Butcher battles on despite suffering a badly gashed head in the vital game against relegation rivals Oxford at Portman Road in April 1986. Butcher scored one of Town's goals in a 3–2 win. Three years later, Butcher would again cut his head, this time more famously, in a World Cup Qualifier against Sweden. He ended the game with his white England shirt soaked in blood, thereby establishing himself as a true English sporting hero.

1985-86: The dreaded drop

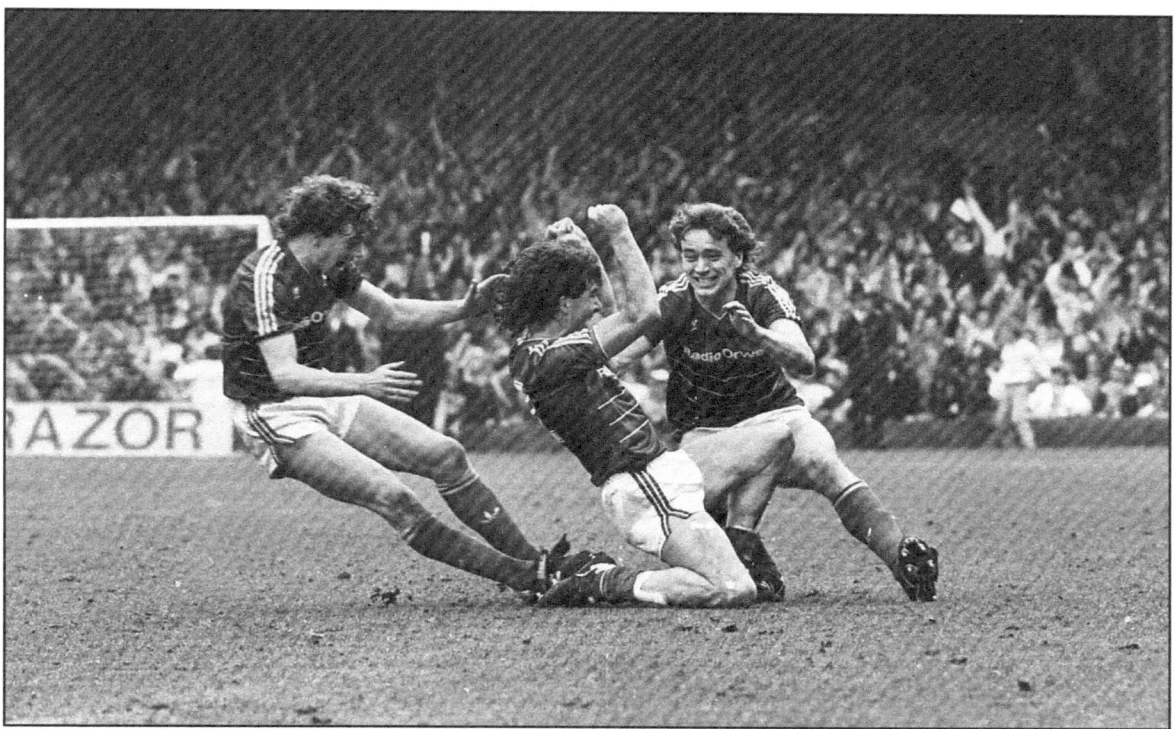

Delirium at Portman Road as Ian Atkins' late, deflected free-kick somehow finds its way into the back of the Oxford net to clinch a drama-filled 3–2 victory for Town over their relegation rivals in April 1986. It wasn't enough, though. Ipswich lost their last two games and Oxford sneaked past them to safety. Town's long, proud 18-season stay in the top flight was ending.

We thought we were safe – but sadly we were wrong. Town fans and players celebrate after the dramatic 3–2 victory over relegation rivals at Oxford at Portman Road in April 1986. Ian Atkins grabbed the winner with a deflected free-kick in the last minute. It would all end in tears.

Hysteria in the stands at Portman Road as Town beat Oxford in the last home game of the 1985–86 season. But we were all celebrating too soon...

We thought we were safe...Town have just beaten Oxford 3–2 in an incredibly dramatic game in April 1986 and ecstatic fans invade the pitch. Sadly, less than two weeks later, Ipswich were relegated.

1985-86: The dreaded drop

Terry Butcher receives his Player of the Year award before the game against Oxford at Portman Road in April 1986. No one knew it at the time, but this was to be Butcher's last game at Portman Road. Although Town won 3–2 in dramatic style – with Butcher among the goalscorers – Ipswich lost their last two games of the season and were relegated after 18 seasons in the top-flight. Butcher was soon on his way to Glasgow Rangers.

1986-87: Play-off disappointment

After a decent season back in Division Two, Ipswich qualified for the new-fangled Play-offs – the beginning of a long love-hate relationship! – but lost to Charlton over two legs.

Kevin Wilson once again topped the goalscoring charts with an impressive 21 to help ensure a top five finish for Town, albeit some distance behind the top two of Derby and Portsmouth.

It was the final season at Ipswich for Paul Cooper, the last link with 1981, and he bowed in typical style with six penalty saves, including one in the first leg of the Play-off.

Town suffered defeat by Birmingham in the third round of the FA Cup, and were beaten by Cambridge in the third round of the Littlewoods Cup.

Bobby Ferguson's contract was not renewed at the end of the season – the first time this had happened to a Town manager.

Division Two final position: Fifth
FA Cup: Third round
Littlewoods Cup: Third round

Back in the Second Division after 18 years, Town's new reduced circumstances are emphasised by the arrival of Grimsby for the first game of the season. It ends 1–1, Kevin Wilson putting Town ahead, they concede a late equaliser.

Ipswich are back in the Second Division for the first time in 18 years, and they don't make a good start. After two draws, they lose their third game of the season, 1–0 at home to Oldham. Here, stalwart 'keeper Paul Cooper collects a cross.

Town striker Mich D'Avray climbs highest in this attack against Shrewsbury in September 1986. The South African scored the only goal of the game.

Visitors Shrewsbury proved less than attractive opposition when they came to Portman Road in August 1986. Fewer than 10,000 fans bothered to turn out to watch Town's 1–0 win, courtesy of this goal from Mich D'Avray.

Temper, temper. Two Scunthorpe defenders seem to be having a mild disagreement as Mark Brennan celebrates his goal in this Littlewoods Cup game at Portman Road in October 1986. Town won the game 2–0 and the two-leg tie 4–1 on aggregate. It didn't exactly stir the blood – only 6,587 diehards turned out to watch.

Mich D'Avray celebrates scoring the only goal of the game against Brighton at Portman Road in October 1986. The South African striker was in Town's first team squad for 10 years, but never really established himself as regular.

A determined Dalian Atkinson bursts past the Brighton defence in one of his first Town games. Atkinson would establish himself as a firm favourite with his astonishing pace and habit of scoring specatcular goals.

1986-87: Play-off disappointment

Nigel Gleghorn holds off a Brighton opponent during Town's 1–0 home win in October 1986.

Nigel Gleghorn is beaten to the ball by a Huddersfield opponent during this game at Portman Road in November 1986. But Gleghorn and his teammates ran out comfortable 3–0 winners, thanks to goals from Ian Atkins and two from John Deehan.

Kevin 'Jockey' Wilson is sent flying by a Huddersfield defender in a 3–0 Ipswich win in November 1986. Wilson wasn't on target in this game, but he did score more than 20 goals in the season to help secure a Play-off spot. The scorers in this game were John Deehan with two, and Ian Atkins.

Kevin Wilson and John Deehan were a decent striking partnership, scoring 32 goals between them in 1986–87. Here they are, looking for chances in the home game against Barnsley in November 1986. Wilson scored the only goal of the game.

1986-87: Play-off disappointment

What a great servant Micky Stockwell was. Here he is in one of his early games for Town, in the victory over Barnsley in 1986. Stockwell was still at Portman Road 14 years later, before moving down the A12 to Colchester.

Defender Tony Humes tries a specatcular effort during Town's 4–1 win at Reading in December 1986. Kevin Wilson and Mark Brennan both scored twice. The stadium is the rather dilapidated Elm Park, soon to be replaced by the Madjeski Stadium.

It looks pretty packed, but only 10,000 fans watched Ipswich beat Barnsley in November 1986, thanks to Kevin Wilson's goal.

Kevin Wilson grabbed two goals as Town beat Reading 4–1 at Elm Park in December 1986. Mark Brennan scored the other two. Wilson had a great season, finishing with 21 goals as Town made the Play-offs.

A rare shot of Michael Cole in an Ipswich shirt. The striker never really established himself in the first team. He and his teammates made a good start to 1987, winning 2–0 against Leeds on New Year's Day, courtesy of goals from Romeo Zondervan and Nigel Gleghorn.

Romeo Zondervan puts Ipswich ahead against Leeds on New Year's Day 1987 – the Dutchman's only goal of the season. It was a happy first day of the year for Ipswich fans, as Nigel Gleghorn was also on target in a 2–0 win.

Spot the fans! Just over 10,000 turn out to watch Ipswich beat Bradford 1–0 in March 1987, courtesy of John Deehan.

Ian Cranson is beaten to this cross by the Bradford 'keeper, but Town won this Division Two game in March 1987 1–0, thanks to a strike from John Deehan, who is also seen in this picture.

Come on, ref…John Deehan doesn't look a happy chappie during Town's game against Brighton in March 1987. He was smiling at the end, though, as late goals from Kevin Wilson and Mich D'Avray saw the visitors snatch a dramatic 2–1 victory.

Which way am I going? Frank Yallop tries to fool a Brighton defender during Town's visit to the south coast in March 1987. The Seagulls went ahead but Kevin Wilson equalised and Mich D'Avray scored a dramatic last minute winner. The chap leaning against the fence seems less than enthralled!

After arriving from arch-rivals Norwich City, John Deehan enjoyed some success at Portman Road. Here he is, battling away against the Hull defence in a dour goalless draw at Portman Road in March 1987.

Mark Brennan tries to burst clear of the Hull defence, but this game at Portman Road in March 1987 ended goalless.

Millwall adopted, ahem, uncompromising tactics to keep Ipswich at bay when they came to Portman Road in April 1987. The game ended 0–0. Here, Town striker Kevin Wilson is brought down.

1986-87: Play-off disappointment

Ipswich fans endured their first taste of Play-off heartbreak at the end of the 1986–87 season – there would be plenty more to come! After finishing fifth in Division Two, Ipswich were pitted against First Division strugglers Charlton. The first leg at Portman Road finished goalless, with Paul Cooper saving a penalty. At the Valley, Ipswich conceded two early goals and Charlton ran out 2–1 winners. Here is Mark Brennan in action in the first leg.

The beginning of Ipswich Town's love-hate relationship with the Play-offs. Charlton were their opponents at the end of the 1986–87 season, and after this goalless draw at Portman Road, the Londoners won the second leg 2–1.

Ian Atkins wasn't the most cultured of players, but you could never criticise his commitment. The fans appreciated his efforts, and here he is picking up a Player of the Year trophy at the end of the 1986–87 season.

Romeo Zondervan proudly shows off his trophy after being voted the Supporters' Player of the Year in the 1986–87 season.

1987-88: Duncan era begins

The arrival of new manager John Duncan failed to perk up Town's fortunes. They finished a disappointing eighth, a distant 11 points outside the Play-off zone. Ten defeats in a miserable 14-game run after Christmas wrecked any hopes of promotion.

New signing David Lowe finished as top scorer with 18 goals, with a decent contribution from the powerful and pacy Dalian Atkinson.

There was a significant return in the form of old hero John Wark, a popular move with fans.

In the FA Cup, Town were unlucky to lose by the odd goal in three at home to Manchester United in the third round, while they reached the fourth round of the Littlewoods Cup before going out to Luton.

Division Two final position: Eighth
FA Cup: Third round
Littlewoods Cup: Fourth round

Shirt-sleeve order for the first game of the new 1987–88 season as Town take on Aston Villa – two great sides from the early 1980s now in reduced circumstances. Villa go ahead through a Chris O'Donnell own-goal, but Nigel Gleghorn equalises. Here he is, celebrating while Villa 'keeper Nigel Spink and his defenders look less than amused.

Former fireman Nigel Gleghorn produced some decent displays for Ipswich in the late 1980s. He lacked pace but had some tricks up his sleeve and knew where the goal was. He scored Town's goal in this 1–1 draw against Aston Villa in the opening game of the 1987–88 season. This was John Duncan's first game in charge.

David Lowe (number seven) wheels away in triumph after scoring the only goal of the game against Leeds in September 1987.

1987-88: Duncan era begins

Mark Brennan celebrates his spectacular goal against Swindon in Town's 3–2 win over the Robins in September 1987.

Romeo Zondervan in action against Swindon in September 1987. Town won this one 3–2, with Frank Yallop (penalty), Mark Brennan, and Mich D'Avray on target.

Hard man Ian Cranson shows his battle scars as Town take on Barnsley in October 1987. Ipswich won the game thanks to David Lowe's goal.

It looks more like ballet than football as David Lowe tries to outwit a Barnsley opponent at Portman Road in October 1987. Lowe scored the winner.

1987-88: Duncan era begins

David Lowe shows his frustration as Town fail to score in this Littlewoods Cup tie against Southend in October 1987. Ipswich did win the game 1–0, with Graham Harbey the unlikely scorer.

There have been some pretty awful away kits over the years, but this strip sported by Huddersfield when they came to Portman Road in November 1987 must be a strong contender for the worst! The Terriers went back to Yorkshire with their tails between their legs, losing 3–0 to goals from Neil Woods, David Lowe and Mark Brennan.

David Lowe lets fly with his left foot in the 3–0 win over Huddersfield in November 1987.

1987-88: Duncan era begins

159

Ipswich pair Jason Dozzell and David Lowe challenge for the ball with Luton's Mal Donaghy in this fourth round Littlewoods Cup tie in November 1987. Donaghy and his defensive partner Steve Foster frustrate the home side, and Luton go through thanks to Brian Stein's goal.

Mich D'Avray in typical aerial action as Town take on Joe Royle's Oldham in November 1987. Ipswich overcame the Latics, with goals from Mark Brennan and David Lowe.

David Lowe celebrates after putting Town ahead against Crystal Palace at Portman Road on Boxing Day 1987. 'Keeper George Wood doesn't look happy. But it wasn't a happy Christmas for Ipswich – they lost this game 3–2 eventually.

It's not a classic, but it's in the back of the net and that's what matters. Town are heading for a 2–1 win over Stoke on New Year's Day 1988, with goals from David Lowe and Mich D'Avray.

Action from a 2–1 win at Stoke on New Year's Day 1988. David Lowe is seen scoring one of the Ipswich goals. Mich D'Avray got the other. More interesting are some of the other characters in this photograph, incuding former Town hero Brian Talbot in the background, and Lee Dixon, chasing back in an unsuccessful attempt to keep Lowe's shot out of the net. Oh, and the legendary George Berry, of course.

David Lowe tangles with a Millwall defender during a 1–1 draw at Portman Road in January 1988. Mich D'Avray put Town ahead in the 75th minute, only for Tony Cascarino to level with virtually the last kick of the game.

1987-88: Duncan era begins

Mich D'Avray beats Colin Hendry to this header but Town are heading to a defeat against Blackburn in January 1988.

Steady on! This doesn't look a very clever challenge on Frank Yallop as Town take on Blackburn in January 1988. The northerners won 2–0.

Warky's still going strong! Here's the veteran in aerial action against Leeds at Elland Road in February 1988. Town lost 1–0. Having made his debut way back in 1975, Wark didn't play his final Town game until November 1996, an amazing 21-year Ipswich career in three spells.

Mick Stockwell was a fantastic servant for Ipswich, always giving 100 per cent wherever he played – full-back, midfield, even striker for a spell! Here he is, in action against Leeds in a 1–0 defeat at Elland Road in February 1988.

Battling Ian Cranson had the unenviable task of replacing legendary Terry Butcher in the number-six shirt. While lacking Butcher's pedigree, he did share his warrior-like qualities – as he shows here against Leicester City in February 1988. He's even sporting a trademark Butcher head bandage! Town lost this game 2–0.

Town are sliding to a fifth consecutive defeat as Leicester come to Portman Road in February 1988, the visitors winning 2–0. Graham Harbey is the Town player in the foreground. He was never destined to become a Portman Road legend.

Ian Atkins has to literally dig the ball out on an uncharacteristically poor-looking Portman Road pitch as Town take on Plymouth in February 1988. John Deehan puts Ipswch ahead, but the Devon side bounce back to win 2–1.

1987-88: Duncan era begins

Disgruntled fans were deserting Town by the time Hull City came to Portman Road in March 1988. The empty seats tell their own story – only 9,728 supporters bothered to turn out for this one. The stay-away supporters missed a 2–0 Ipswich win, with goals from Neil Woods and David Lowe.

It's March 1988, Hull are the visitors at Portman Road and Town are heading for their first home win since Christmas. A rare goal from Neil Woods and another from David Lowe, seen celebrating here, are crucial.

1987-88: Duncan era begins

Town's two goalscorers against Hull City in March 1988. David Lowe has just made the game safe for Ipswich, and is congratulated by fellow striker Neil Woods, who had put Ipswich ahead early in the game.

A low point – a home defeat to Bournemouth in front of only 10,208 diehard fans in March 1988. Here, Town successfully defend a Cherries corner. Neil Woods got Town's goal in a 2–1 loss to a team managed by a certain Harry Redknapp.

The legendary Ipswich Town 'Memory Man' Ron Ellis watches at the Town team run out for the game against Bournemouth in March 1988. Ron's memory for everything Ipswich Town was extraordinary: he would ask your birth date and then tell you the result of the game closest to the day of your arrival, the teams, the scorers, and probably the names of everyone in the crowd! Sadly missed.

A rare highlight in a dull season. Middlesbrough are put to the sword at Portman Road in April 1988, with Town scoring four without reply. Mich D'Avray is seen celebrating his goal, with Simon Milton, but the star of the show is hat-trick hero Dalian Atkinson. Future Town skipper Tony Mowbray is in the visitors' defence.

Frank Yallop with his Player of the Year trophy at the end of the 1987–88 season. Right-back Yallop was a loyal servant for Ipswich over the years, and weighed in with some spectacular goals.

'Mercurial' is the only way to describe Dalian Atkinson – brilliant one moment, awful the next. One of his good days came in this game against Birmingham in the final home game of the 1987–88 season, when he scored the only goal with a cheeky back-heel.

1988-89: Treading water

In John Duncan's second season, Town again finished eighth, albeit only three points outside the Play-offs this time.

A highlight is the arrival of Sergei Baltacha, the first Soviet to play in English football. Baltacha thrilled Town fans with a goal on his debut, but manager Duncan mystifyingly didn't play him at sweeper, the position where he won 45 caps for a very strong USSR side!

Joint top of the goalscoring charts with 13 was a familiar face, John Wark, who shared the top spot with Dalian Atkinson. Jason Dozzell contributed 12, with former Bury Town player Simon Milton weighing in with 10.

The gulf which had developed between Ipswich and the top teams was made painfully obvious with two heavy Cup defeats: 6–2 to Aston Villa in the Littlewoods Cup, and 3–0 to Nottingham Forest in the FA Cup.

Division Two final position: Eighth

FA Cup: Third round

Littlewoods Cup: Fourth round

For a short spell, Dalian Atkinson was superb for Ipswich. Here's the mercurial one celebrating after putting Town ahead against Sunderland in the first home game of the 1988–89 season. Ipswich won 2–0, Jason Dozzell getting the other one.

1988-89: Treading water

An early season thriller saw Town edge out Watford 3–2 at Portman Road in September 1988. Here, players and fans are celebrating one of the goals, which came from Simon Milton, Dalian Atkinson and David Lowe.

Craig Forrest collects the ball safely as Town see off visitors Manchester City 1–0 thanks to a Jason Dozzell goal in October 1988. But it was Manchester City, and not Ipswich, who would go up at the end of the season.

Glum faces as Ipswich concede a goal against Swindon at the County Ground in November 1988. In fact, the Robins were two goals to the good with only 23 minutes left, but an amazing late comeback from Town saw them score three goals to win the game. The first came from Dalian Atkinson, but Ipswich were still behind with only three minutes remaining before strikes from Jason Dozzell and Romeo Zondervan proved decisive.

He's behind you, Romeo! Town's Zondervan is chased by Chelsea hard man Graham Roberts during a 3–0 defeat at Stamford Bridge on Boxing Day 1988. Chelsea end up as Division Two champions.

1988-89: Treading water

Sergei Baltacha signs autographs for young fans on his arrival at Ipswich in early 1989. The name Baltacha is still famous – but in tennis circles these days, of course. Elena, Sergei's daughter, is Britain's number one woman tennis player.

Sergei Baltacha with Town boss John Duncan after signing for Town in 1989. One of football's great mysteries: Why did Duncan sign a Soviet with dozens of caps for the USSR as a sweeper, and then play him in midfield?

IPSWICH TOWN The 1980s

An historic moment in English football: USSR sweeper Sergei Baltacha becomes the first Soviet to play in this country. He is welcomed by Ipswich captain Romeo Zondervan in January 1989. They don't exactly look overjoyed, do they? Perhaps they already know about manager John Duncan's masterplan of playing Baltacha on the right side of midfield. Can anyone explain that?

Sergei Baltacha challenges for the ball during his memorable Town debut against Stoke at Portman Road in January 1989. The Soviet nets his only Ipswich goal in a 5–1 win, but things go downhill after that.

Sergei Baltacha is congratulated by teammates after scoring on his Ipswich debut against Stoke at Portman Road in January 1989. He gets a hug from skipper Romeo Zondervan and Jason Dozzell is about to join in the celebrations. The disconsolate Stoke number four is none other than Chris Kamara, now a Sky Sports TV pundit.

1988-89: Treading water

A thriller at Walsall in January 1989. Town win 4–2, with five of the goals coming in a mad 13-minute spell early in the second half. This picture shows Jason Dozzell scoring the second Ipswich goal from close range. John Wark, Chris Kiwomya and Ian Redford were also on target.

No chance, Chris! Diminutive Chris Kiwomya loses this aerial challenge in the 2–1 home defeat at the hands of Crystal Palace in February 1989. Ian Wright – whatever happened to him? – scored both Palace goals, with John Wark getting Town's consolation.

An afternoon to forget at Maine Road. Town are thumped 4–0 by Manchester City in February 1989. Here, Frank Yallop and John Wark battle away in a losing cause.

Spot the ball! A right old tangle during Town's 4–0 defeat at Manchester City in February 1989.

1988-89: Treading water

It's a mystery, as Toyah would warble. The player to the far right of the picture, facing away from the camera and apparently trying to fly-hack the ball, seems to be Ipswich 'keeper Ron Fearon. This is a Division Two game against Shrewsbury in March 1989. Fearon's antics didn't do any damage – Ipswich won 2–0, with Dalian Atkinson getting both of them.

Simon Milton tries his luck as Chelsea come to Portman Road in March 1989. Gordon Durie's late goal wins the game for the eventual Division Two champions.

It's 14 years since his debut, and Warky is still knocking them in! Here, the veteran has just scored the first in a 3–1 win against Bournemouth in March 1989. He was playing as a makeshift striker at this point. Dalian Atkinson got Town's other two.

David Linighan was a solid, if unsophisticated, centre-half for Town for a number of seasons. Here he is, in typically uncompromising action, against Hull City in April 1989. This game ended 1–1, with Hull's Swan contributing the Ipswich goal.

A rare goal from Romeo Zondervan during Town's demolition of Birmingham in April 1989. The Blues won 4–0, with David Lowe scoring two and John Wark also on target.

1989-90: Fans turn on the boss

Town's normally patient fans showed their unhappiness with John Duncan as Ipswich spluttered their way to ninth place, missing the Play-offs for a third consecutive season. It was as much the style of play as the results which caused supporters to lose patience.

Duncan lost his job at the end of the campaign after three lacklustre seasons.

David Lowe was back on top of the goalscoring charts with 13, with significant contributions also coming from Simon Milton, John Wark, and the consistent Jason Dozzell.

These were unhappy times for Town fans, with home attendances slumping below 10,000 on occasions.

There was no joy in the Cups, either, with Ipswich losing to Tranmere in the second round of the Littlewoods Cup, and a defeat to Barnsley in the fourth round of the FA Cup.

Division Two final position: Ninth
FA Cup: Fourth round
Littlewoods Cup: Second round

A study of David Linighan. Linighan was an effective, if uncomplicated, centre-back.

Wwoods wasn't one of John Duncan's better captures. Here he is, battling away against Oxford in the autumn of 1989.

One of Town's best cut-price captures in the 1980s was that of Simon Milton from Bury Town. Here he is, playing against Oxford in 1989. Town came back from 2–0 to grab a point in this game, with Ian Redford and an own-goal earning them a draw.

Mich D'Avray celebrates with Town fans after putting Ipswich ahead against Stoke in September 1989. The game ended 2–2, with Jason Dozzell the other scorer for the home side.

A screamer from Jason Dozzell puts Ipswich 2–0 up against Mick Mills' Stoke in September 1989. Mich D'Avray had scored the first. Despite being 2–0 up at half-time, Town let it slip and Stoke got a draw.

Mich D'Avray is thwarted by the Newcastle defence as Town entertain the Toon in October 1989, but goals from John Wark and David Lowe ensured a 2–1 Town win.

David Lowe scored one of Town's goals in a 2–1 win over visitors Newcastle in October 1989. Lowe never gave less than 100 per cent – and he grabbed more than a few goals into the bargain.

One good move from John Duncan was the signing of former nappy salesman (do you think he's just a little bit fed up with being called that?) Neil Thompson. A solid left-back with a thunderous shot, Thompson is seen here in action against Bradford.

Chria Kiwomya was on target twice as Ipswich overcame visitors Plymouth 3–0 in October 1989. Simon Milton was the other scorer. Here's goal hero Kiwomya in athletic action.

Ipswich beat Watford 4–1 in the second round of the barely-remembered Zenith Data Systems Cup at Portman Road in November 1989. David Gregory helped himself to a hat-trick, and Ian Redford got the other. Here, Neil Woods holds off Glenn Roeder.

David Lowe is looking the wrong way, but the reaction from the home fans tells us that he's just scored one of Town's goals in a 3–1 victory against West Brom in November 1989. David Lowe and Simon Milton got the others.

Town players in the defensive wall look round anxiously to see 'keeper Craig Forrest make a spectacular save from this West Brom free-kick at Portman Road in November 1989. Ipswich won 3–1.

Gavin Johnson battles for the ball against West Brom during Town's 3–1 win at Portman Road in November 1989. Local boy Johnson had a fantastic career in both professional and local football.

Tony Humes didn't score a lot of goals for Town, but there's one spectacular one against Middlesbrough in December 1989. Town won 3–0, with Mick Stockwell and Louie Donowa also on the scoresheet. This game brought down the curtain on the 1980s for Ipswich Town. It was a decade which began so gloriously, with the capture of the UEFA Cup during what was almost certainly Town's greatest season. But it all slipped away so quickly: within the blink of an eye Robson had gone, the great team had broken up, and Ipswich were in the Second Division.